LIFTED

Comeback Poetry for a Needed Time

Kristy Hellum

authorHOUSE®

AuthorHouse™
1663 Liberty Drive
Bloomington, IN 47403
www.authorhouse.com
Phone: 1 (800) 839-8640

Published by AuthorHouse 04/23/2018

ISBN: 978-1-5462-3416-6 (sc)
ISBN: 978-1-5462-3414-2 (hc)
ISBN: 978-1-5462-3415-9 (e)

Library of Congress Control Number: 2018903454

Print information available on the last page.

Someone take firmly

no, tenderly

my shoulders

and give them a little shake

and say;

beautifully done

this

breaking open.

KH

PREFACE

Dear Reader,

There is a force in human consciousness that mystics and poets often call *God*, which in truth has many names. Scattered amongst the leaves of poetry in this collection, you shall encounter these variations:

Immeasurable Universe, Mystery, Beauty, Love, Spirit, Beloved and *One.*

My deep heart's desire is that you will allow yourself to exchange the name of One for another, to better suit your unique beliefs and soulful life. Stir all the variations together, add honey, sip while reading. Be surprised how deliciously the tastebuds can absorb a multitude of new flavors.

May it be so;
That *We The People*
having studied our history of inquisitions
and having witnessed first hand
the tragedies of enslavement and brutality
in the name of a supreme being,

Can and will
in this lifetime
celebrate the extinction
of hate and intolerance
justified by any doctrine

May we never again,
feel the need to constrict our minds
nor cower our hearts
when hearing this one word;
God

May it be so

With Love and Blessings,
Kristy

Ocean waves of deep gratitude

To these inspirational readers, witnesses, poets, gifters
of insight and creative souls who said yes and yes
again through the journey there and back again.

Evan Hodkins - Soulfriend and mentor, my parents Ginger Gray and
Frank Hellum, Kathy Hellum - photographer and sister, my teachers/
children - Georgia Ruth and Forrest Gray, Tamam Kahn - first poetry
teacher, June Elhers, Ruthie Schnable Turbidy, Shana Langer, Kathie
Kelly, L'aura Reneau, Jeri Bee, Azure Kurth, Mirabai Joni Stemple,
Tommilou Robinson Davison, Mary H. Cummings, Michael Furniss,
Pamela Challender, Kelly Lay-Raitt, Nica Pozanovich, Judy Brannan
Armbruster, Aleta Greenspan, Lee Brewster, Terra Pearson, Vicki Marie
Stolsen, Cindi Smith Kaup, Twana Sparks, Jill Brady, Doug Von Koss,
Larry Robinson, Deva Davida Gordon, Marlene Allen, Myah Allen,
Kate Schuyler, Pippa Breakspear, Stephani-Lila Murdoch, Helah
Blumhagen, Kirsten Hartlein Allen, Liesl Jobson, Perry Pike, Bhavani
Judith Cook Tucker, The Institute of Imaginal Studies (Meridian
University), Murshida Mariam Baker and all my Path of the Heart
Sufi brothers and sisters who swim in the poetry of Rumi and each
other everyday.

CONTENTS

Now Is The Needed Time - lyrics

Now is the needed time
I'm down on my bended knees
I'm on my knees, a prayin'
Won't you come, come by here?

Even if you don't stay long,
Even if you don't stay long,
I'm prayin' won't you
Come by here

traditional gospel spiritual

WON'T YOU COME BY HERE

Cup Your Hands

Find a teacher,
preferably one that lives
close by
very close,
like inside

Then build a container
you don't have to cut down a tree
letting the wood season all year
in the forest or buy a lathe
or sign up for a wood turning class

All you have to do is
cup your hands,
they become their own container
your sacred bowl

Now whisper a prayer
into those cupped hands,
they hold all the prayers
you have yet to pray

If you do not know how to pray
simply say to yourself:
thank you, a thousand
or eight thousand times

If you wonder who you're praying to
don't worry,
everyone wonders this
most of the time

The rabbi while reciting a blessing
The monk while sipping tea
The pilgrim walking tired to the next village

Please please please
thank you thank you thank you
or the other way around
it doesn't matter which comes first;

      A teacher
      A container
      Prayer or
      Gratitude.

Why

Honest poetry
like great works of art
is the *only* thing
that has *helped me* **stop lying** to myself
it makes *forgiveness* seem simple
it replaces denial with a **tolerable** awe
it makes *suffering*
almost
worthwhile.

Forgiveness

Forgiveness was just
   not my cup of tea,
      instead I was searching
         for something more profound

It must be deeper than that
It must be deeper than this

Stop trying to understand
   how you survived the time
      when the sacred was torn
         from your heart

End your collusion with forgiveness
It is really God doing all the work anyway.

Norwegian Grandfathers

My grandfather lived under the viaduct,
Seattle's modern Skid Row
Salt air softened his dark face;

    Eyes like the Aleut
    Cheekbones like the Chinook

He drank under the viaduct
fast and furious
like the trucks
rumbling on concrete above his head

He was the underground Seattle
one of its dark knights
He ate smoked fish
that scented his jacket
the day we met

    Brown eyes like mine
    Round face like mine
    Missing teeth like mine

I was six when we found him
our father driving four curious children
to meet the quiet man, our grandfather
who out of respect
wore a gray suit that hung limp
on bent-over bones

Our grandfather living on Skid Row
descendants of the logging men
the fishermen
the failed gold miners
the daring men
who once sailed here
from Oslo

　　Who knew the sea
　　Who knew the salmon
　　Who knew how to shape logs into homes
　　and children's bed boards

Grandfathers all of them
who slept outside now
smelling of salt brine
aroma of the Puget Sound

　　He lived near the sea
　　Drank near the sea
　　Died near the sea

Norwegian eyes like the Snohomish
Quinault, his forehead
the Athabaskan face
of lost men.

At the Door

There are periods
in life where hopefully so
I get to meet
the part of me
that is so
splendidly needy
so
exquisitely
inadequate

Oh let me greet her
with doors
wide open
there is nothing
to protect me
from my
shadow
in this
being single.

Sunflower

Watch now
how the sunflower turns
its head all day
just to catch
another glimpse

Watch now
how the silver light
dances at night
following you close

Feel yourself
caressed by the moon
be the sunflower
willing to kneel and kiss the ground

Then turn
so you face
what loves you
most.

The Great Divide

Dear 11,000 foot Rocky Mountain meadow
Dear cobalt dragonfly
Dear aspen shimmer
Dear bare breasted meditation
Dear pastures of Elk
Dear dark mirror lake

Dear altitude sickness
Dear dehydration headache
Dear obnoxious hikers with cell phones
Dear tragedy I'm running from
Dear empty bank account
Dear out of control tortured worry thoughts.....

Wait! Excuse me?!
In the middle of all this beauty?
Can we get back to where we were?

Dear 11,000 foot Rocky Mountain meadow
Dear cobalt dragonfly
Dear aspen shimmer...

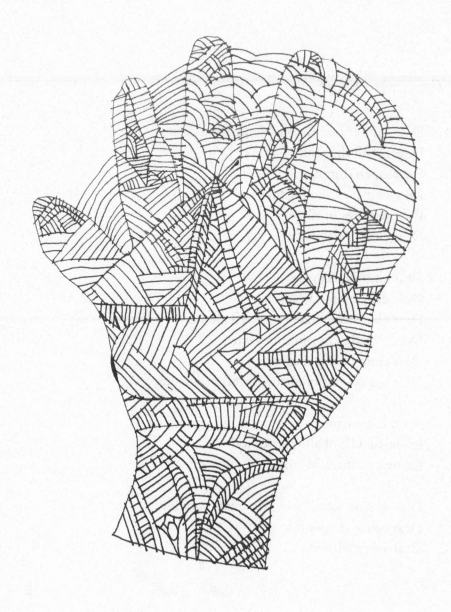

Trisomy 21

I love a man with rashes blotting his arms
and acne dotting his back
with toenails growing out of control and
teeth as crooked as his smile

He is a delight
He is lovely
He is so kind
Does not know how to insult

I love a man who always
buttons his shirt to the top
It looks kind of silly but
he thinks it's cool and kinda
old school

He sings off key but with
reverence and sincerity

He loves to play poker and
often takes the pot

I'm not much of a gambler
but I will place all my bets
on this man's enduring heart

I love a man who eats too much
drinks too much and
who doesn't do his dishes.....for days

I keep loving him though
I find him absolutely hilarious
He gives the best toasts at parties
and offers brilliant film critiques

Sure I get annoyed and sharp tongued-
life is better when I stop telling him
that he isn't doing it right and stop
trying to get him to eat more salad

He writes me love notes and creates
epic poetry and paints canvasses with
hearts and hands on them

Born with a little something extra;
a chromosome

He is one of a kind
He is my son.

My Sleepless Night

When I go to the deep shadow cave
The cave of wonders
I meet the troll
What I am
That person?

I was Aladdin on a fine magic carpet ride
The Gods need dreams - I just picked the future
It will begin now
The past will light my way

Take my breath to shooting stars
Shine in my heart, the dark night sky
And it won't be the last likes of me
Again I need to sleep now.

written by Forrest Gray
(Son of the Author, 32 year old artist, born with Down Syndrome)

Trying To Save Myself From Myself

I have taken a lover: Poetry
Have you ever been staggered by a phrase?
She keeps me up all night
I am exhausted from revealing
my innermost secrets

She lures my abandoned parts
to lie down, exposed
next to her
beauty

I will fall in love with someone
who loves the Mystery
as much as I do

This is not over -
I've got unfinished business
with the profound.

FOR A NEEDED TIME

A Poetic Argument For Grief

Take your grief seriously
Become the ash urn
for the vanishing wilderness
Despair for the Dolphins

Make your own salt water
for the disappearing marshes
Be called to outrageous acts of despair
The silent Earth is listening

And then
every now and again,
In the face of splendor,
Turn towards it.

A Healing Contract

When chaos erupts
may sanity prevail in our nation
keep asking;
what do you
dearly love?

When chaos erupts
may we depend on Beauty
and remember the healing contract
we made with poetry

The intimacy of light in the morning has your name on it
seek sanctuary with the salmon
waiting under black
shadowed ledges

When chaos erupts
may we depend on each other
keep asking;
what do you
dearly love?

This Is Not Trivial

When prayers and good thoughts
    are not enough

When a moment of silence and a flag
    half-mast seem irrelevant

When sending best wishes
When hoping
When donating to a cause
When singing in a choir
    lift your spirit only for a moment

When crying alone
    in your kitchen
Serves no one, not even you

May kindness be offered
    on the passing plate
May we smile lovingly still
    into the tired eyes of the man
    holding a cardboard sign
May we dare allow the sad sad news
    that penetrates the fortress of longing
    to melt like an altar candle
    lit for one day's peace

May we remember and trust in this,
our human goodness
and count ourselves;
    fortunate enough
    healthy enough
    alive enough

To have this poem
Touching us
Right now

We can make every breath matter
We can forgive outrageously one more person today
We can look out
From our doorway, and say
Yes -
I am here, I am here
Is there any other way to fight?
This is not trivial:
LOVE

It Matters.

Dear Young People

Speak the truth
As if your life depends on it -
Because it does

Make justice visible
When everything shatters
It's marching time again

In this darkness
Your truth telling matters
It's singing time again

Speak the truth
As if your life depends on it -
Because it does.

The Day After the Election Blues

I'm gonna write me a poem
to stir the woeful air
someday maybe
it'll be a prayer

I'm gonna find a bottle
of something strong
then me and this ol' guitar
gonna turn it into song

Perhaps too bluesy
for my own good
it'll sound just the way
a redemption song should

I'm gonna get me a canvas
big empty and wide
colors and shapes
will erupt from inside

I will not wait for a recount
will not listen to news
just feel the sad
and keep singing the blues.

Recall

I am trying to recall those
hope filled times when the
lilacs knew exactly when to bloom
and the figs always produced in the same months

I could count on those like
grandmother's steady voice
or mother's sturdy hands
when we knew we would be safe,
or
safe enough

Even after that terrible earthquake
when the chimney bricks tumbled down
Even when a father's anger could feel
like the entire house would crumble

I am trying to recall those times
when I could still cry out and
softly someone would touch my cheek

When civility mattered
When leaders were dignified
When our whole house
of a nation felt safe,
or
safe enough

Even after terrible fires, floods and shootings
when tragedy stirs up a mighty compassion

I am trying to recall those times
when we could lie out
all day, exposed
warming ourselves
in the truth of a sun

       Underbelly safe atop
       a large solid boulder
       overlooking the precipice
       just ahead.

Re-run

When did "liberal'
become a dirty word?
If subterfuge is necessary
then let's add a little
mischief making. You and I,
we are good at this.

This is a re-run

You and I, we had
our bright and shining
our Camelot moment, when
everything was fresh
and possible

This is a re-run

Do not waste your imagination
such a precious gift
on predictions
of sheer awfulness

Look - the waves are singing!
Look - a friend has cooked
a sumptuous feast!
Look - the tulips trees are dancing!

This is a re-run

You and I,
we risk going mad,
the push and click
of too much
of too fast information
and spin, turn it off
it is not new or news.

Aren't you getting dizzy?
You and I, we still have
our coyote medicine
let's join the resistance
with a little merriment

We CAN
get
the possible
back

This is a re-run.

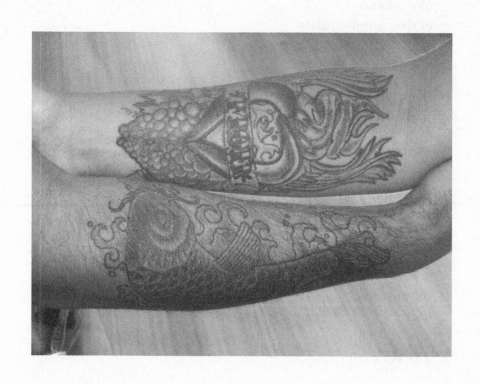

Advice From a Poet Arrested At An Anti-War Protest

I listened to the news
this morning -
by accident

I can tell you the gist:
We may not be a "free nation"
after all

No
It's something entirely different

Get up!
Kiss someone
It may be
your last chance.

To Touch The Anger Within

I glide my nimble fingers
along the blade
squint my eyes
admire work honed
from grief and disbelief
of never ceasing wars

So gentle so soft that tempered edge
a rush of sinew and clear thought
befriends a crouched
mountain lion
living in my belly

This steel, my old friend
holds concise awareness
of the rage portal
I have kept
my foot is wedged
in that door
at the ready

Others have their arsenals;
their brass shells
their gold bars
their rigged elections
I wear my whetted stone
around my neck
like a glistening collar,
a bone and bead choker
to the war dance.

How I Imagine The Pacific Ocean Actually Talking

Standing there
wet with ocean spray
I asked the Pacific Ocean if she would
teach me something -
about anger

"My lover tells me to calm down
and then walks right out of the room,
proclaiming that anger is unnecessary!" I told her.
"Has anyone ever told YOU to calm down?"
I asked.

The basalt rock boomed
beneath my sturdy boots
When the next wave came
crashing upon the cliff
thundering her reply.

In one extravagant swoop
she slapped me hard,
knocking my only pair
of prescription sunglasses
right off my face,
and never
returned them

"There"
she said,
"THAT was necessary"

Refuse to be chained

by story

by deed

by loss

by love

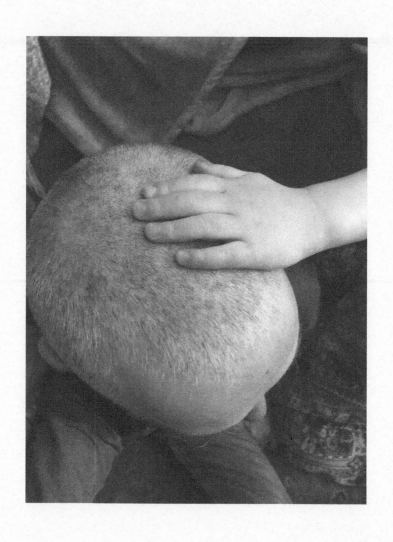

ON MY BENDED KNEE

A Theology of Tears

What can we do with our sorrow?
Each time we cry:

A sacrament of tears
A small baptism

Mourning is my spiritual accomplishment
An outward symbol of an inner grace

Mourning is the art of grieving
It's how I live my life
On behalf of the Universe

Mourning is about not denying grief
It is how I give the Universe an opportunity
To express her grief, through me

Mourning is the origin of singing
The One Song, the Uni Verse

Each time we cry.

Standing Alone In A Redwood Grove

Humbly there
I stood
in foggy shadow
asking about grief

Many thousand year old tree, I asked
hasn't it been enough,
already?

Three hundred feet up
her crowned canopy of branches
danced wildly as
I shivered below
pressing cheek to trunk

Lush layers of redwood duff,
decomposition of moss and fern
confirmed by bare feet
muffled her answer

A shawl of mist
so dense descended
wrapping my shoulders
offering a hushed
grateful reprieve

Thank you
I said

Thank you.

A Particular Sound

Call out
wailing into the wild river
for each night
you loved

Go ahead
expose your outstretched throat
all feral-like
scratch and claw your face
roaring curses to God
do not stop yourself

The rock hard beauty
of this holy grief
unbidden,
disturbs
all hope
of slumber.

Gone Gone

I shut my eyes
many times
I chose to
see only
a future
of us
that
only I
wanted;
I shut my eyes

Now it all gone gone
I take back the things
truly mine;

Like space
on the wide -
very wide
mattress

No more
my side
your side

(here, I sighed)

Now, it all gone, gone,
Now, I take back the entire bed
I take back the entire house
I take back the entirety
of me
I take back the things
truly mine;
      My fire
      My desire
      Truly,

      Mine

No Place For Hate - me

Love can leave its hard impact
like punch bruised ribs
everything dips
below the surface
I by necessity
sank
darkly down
allowed my soul
to plumb the depths
where hate could not be
so there I rested awhile,
immersed in the center of grief's grace

I
am
deeper
than
before.

No Place For Hate - you

Love can leave its hard impact
like bruise punched ribs
everything dips
below the surface
you, by necessity,
sank
darkly down
allowed your soul
to plumb the depths,
where hate could not be
so there, rested awhile
immersed in the center of grief's grace

You
are
deeper
than
before.

Beautiful Gold Fills The Cracks

It's over
leave the shattered shards on the floor
do not bother with a broom, notice
the way the fragments shine
when sunlight creeps
across the room

One day you will sweep up those pieces
when beautiful seams of gold glint
like fractures of ancient vessels,
fill in your spaces of loss
so there will be no chance
of forgetting the
most important
part
of this
journey;

A broken heart has an extraordinary capacity to shine light.

Unbearable Nectar

That midsummer peach
loosely clinging
to its branch
drooping over the neighbor's fence
into
my life

Reaching to touch,
it fell into my hand
that unbearable nectar
oh succulent heartache
an intimate perfection
exposing unbidden
the history of
what was
once
us

The sweetness
still lingering
still holding on

That peach and I
made a bargain;

The only
appropriate response
was to
weep
some more.

Drought Roses

I did not water the roses
growing outside
my bedroom window
that sorrowful summer

Still they grew
leggy and wild
their little rouge dresses
sashaying about
the unruly vines

I tried not to notice
from my silent bed
the fragrance of longing;
Oh! To have them grace
the bedside table
one last time

Sweetly exhausted
from holding on
the tender petals would let go
throughout the night
drifting onto the floor
and I, rising from slumber
would lower my bare feet
to kiss the fresh
rose carpet below,
pressing out
one last and
exquisite
final
sigh.

A Symphony of Mothers

Good people
turn to your mother's
mother's mother

Tell her
you are grateful
for tilling the soul of her people
for your planting

For mothers imprisoned
by bottle
by jail
by hate
by hurt
by church
by marriage

Forgive her
for all the babies
she could not keep
in order she stay
fiercely alive

For servant mothers,
refusing to feel mothers
hell on a pedestal mothers
bruised cheek
under pancake face
mothers

Thank her
for all the children
not hers,
despite protest
she raised
as her own

Good people
let it be known
we are here
to love
our mothers
each one
all.

The Alchemy Of Tragedy

The soot on my kitchen counter
has been wiped clean
except for one section
that I cannot bear to erase

The smoke from the firestorm
filled our homes, the ones
left standing,
leaving precious particles
memories of lives
of dreams ended

Just a fragile layer of dust
enough to keep me
remembering
everyone in
my town

My town
with the thousands of firefighters,
and first responders arriving
from all over this beautiful
country of ours
to help

My town
with the thousands of homes
gone, my town
with fathers and friends
and grandmothers still missing
I will not wipe them clean

Refusing to ask how or who or why
rather I ask myself
only this:
How will this fire transform us?

By the alchemy of tragedy
may the inner story of the fire
keep cracking open
our hearts
Santa Rosa

October 2017

Susan

There was that time late in Spring
when I longed to be her
such stillness
that my hair
instead
would
gently
land

Long and thick as bracelets on the shower floor
a Buddha head, a holy ghost, so beautiful
and tender my mother-sister-friend
laying down her mind to the
inevitability of what
it meant
to say a
good
good

bye
Sweetened was the end
the beauty
of her
release
a simple belief

A summer's falling leaf
too soon
letting
go
.

COMING BACK

COMING BACK

The Way Back

Why is it
I can only trust people
who have had their hearts
broken 101 times or
who have been tortured
in foreign jails
or who have repeated
their time
in rehab
over and over, their
families going broke
or whose life companion
has died in their arms
or whose newborn
arrived still or with
unexpected chromosomes or
those surrounded
by hate and prejudice
(which are the same thing)
yet find ways

to laugh and love
still, who attempt
some form of
forgiving daily
such mean
ignorance?

Perhaps it is because
they did not stop, dreaming
Perhaps it is because
they are the ones
who have come back,
dreaming
still

It is they
who left that
twine along the
labyrinth path
for me to find
my way
back.

Who's Counting

I've lost track of the galaxy count
Like I've stopped counting
Long ago lovers
That five decades has gifted me
Though not all were gifts,
Of course and
Perhaps "lover" is too generous a word;

Conquistador, seducer, love slave, hustler
All those hello goodbye lovers
Sailboat lovers
Cabin in the woods lovers
Ten years of marriage lovers
Lied to lovers
Scoundrel lovers
Many months of bliss lovers
Brokenhearted lovers
And countless...

Did you hear me?
I said countless
exchanges of Light,
exchanges of of trust
of fluid
of strength
of fear
of laughter
of ecstasy
exchanges that pierced deeper and deeper
until I
began
falling
falling
falling
into the arms of an
immeasurable heaven
where I
finally
finally
finally
stopped counting.

A Fragrance From Your Garden

Have you noticed how
Age and wisdom

have been kissing
your face these days?

Moistened by tears
and years of fierce grace

It's pouring through you -
say farewell to prettiness

Such radiance is making the
zinnias and dahlias
tell the gardener,
"We'll have what she's having!"
blooming
all the way
through winter.

Listen

There is a sacred pool

waiting for me

it is the only place

I go true

As I write this

Mockingbird is telling

a story

Shhhhhhhhh

I must listen now.

Under wraps

This morning
in the courtyard
I know you heard it
while hanging out the laundry

Even the Raven and Bluejay
knew the entire song by heart
that deep bass part
atop a sultry alto harmony

As you reached up
clothespin ready
I saw your hip
reply to the air
that caressed
you there

You cannot keep
your shimmy under wraps
one more measure of stillness
may kill you,
so dance.

The Vows We Make

Today I took the ocean
as my lover
exchanging vows
before the crashing surf
could stir it all up all again
making me change my mind

Between the swells
inside the hush
she had been composing
a seduction song all along
to which I surrendered

Willingly I offered myself
to her surf
old sorrows
old stories
spilled out

A holy breaker
a perfect arch
curled over my naked body
an exquisite surge
tumbled me
pummeled me
forward
toward the edge
of her
ecstatic shore.

Love Cannibal

i am a reluctant cannibal;
i feel bad when i do it
when i consume people
or parts of them
it is only to survive
and clearly - you offered

vampires, by comparison
do not believe in consent

anyway
i was saving my own ass
and you were dying.

Table For One Blues

I came here to sit and enjoy myself
To indulge in the fact there ain't no one else

The hostess asked me
"table for two?"
I said "No, I'm plenty of woman,
table for one"

The shape of my hips
The shine on my lips
Don't go thinking you know something about me

The fierce in my eyes
It's my disguise
Don't let that entice you to tame me

The way I slowly take my sip
The way I let this honey drip
Don't keep your hungry eyes on me

I came here to sit and enjoy myself
To indulge in the fact there ain't no one else

The hostess asked me
"table for two?"
I said "No, I'm plenty of woman,
table for one"

Meet Me There (Homage to Rumi)

Shhhhhh…do not speak
let's use our bodies for truth telling-
it's better than arguing in poetic verse
the reasons why we
should or should not
allow our hearts
to be smashed to smithereens
once more

Let's get this over with…
I know blackberry patch
where everything goes wrong…
I'll meet you there

Free yourself from changing me
leave the brambles in my hair and
I promise to let your eyebrows
grow all willy-nilly and
never pluck
a single one.

GIFTS

Things A Sufi May Say To You

Every minute
we are all
getting more beautiful
All the way to heaven
we are healing
Do not lose your magic

Where is your sanctuary?
What tree?
What room?
What body part do you love?
You don't need an entire house
There's a healing space inside of you
let's do a ritual,
together.

Listen. This is your practice
Whatever the composer has written;
Listen.
Play that.
Practice THAT

Keep dreaming
in your night travels
look for more creatures
when you awaken;
you will find them...
and the meaning
of your life

Every
Minute
We
All
Get
More
Beautiful.

Mexico Sufi camp

*"Thank you Asha Greer for sharing your lifetime of inspiration,
artistry and teachings"*

The Dark Feminine

There is a ferocious Diva
living inside the darkness of you
who will not stop singing

You, who have been shown
the secret cave entrance
prepare yourself
for what darkness has to offer

Transforming suffering
into wisdom
may take awhile

Leave the burning flame outside
do not bring a candle
or you will not learn a thing

Greet dark wisdom
with captivating grace
if a priestess offers you her torch
a precious gift,
let it burn through you
the way truth telling does

There is a ferocious Diva
living inside of you.
Go
Into the dark.

Sea Glass

Tossed around
by a tumultuous surf
and with enough time
the shards of your sorrow
have been polished

Turn yourself
into magnificent art

Even shattered glass
becomes precious
to the jewelry maker.

Hello Again

What if I could feel now
as I once did -
an astonishing love wrapped
warmly around me each morning
to feel now
that balm of holy knowing
a joy filled steadfastness
of being held
in sacred promise
to another being
that I could swear by
whose warmth of tender skin
so touched mine with a constancy
that steadied storms and inspired courage?

What if I began today
to laugh and delight in myself instead?
to tease lightly my own foibles
to adore my own aging face
and with gentle fingers
trace my own smile lines
to look deeply into my own eyes
to say aloud one more time -
What a miracle it is to have found you!
and from the depths of awe and wonder
looking back at me in Love's mirror
I would hear,
Yes! What a miracle it is to have
found each other,
again.

Welcome back.

Lifted

There was a time when I
could not let myself
be lifted

curled up on that floor
no imagination of what
could become
my life

pressing against the treachery
of another breath
I heard a gasp - mine
whispering; why? why?

Choking on disbelief
my throat cleared enough
for the sounds that followed

A lonely lament
wounded animal cries
an old negro spiritual
getting louder and louder
pouring out of me
undiluted, threatening
to flood my entire house

in that fetal position of sound
in that throat burning moment
in that rhythmic moaning
I heard a high pitched wailing

from somewhere
both inside
and outside
my mouth

which pierced the translucent sac
around my soul, birthing the moment
when I suddenly knew
what would lift me off that floor;
when I learned
what my sorrow was for

That is when the lamentations
elongated into words
cries became vibrant colors of silk
flowing through swoosh whoosh ink of pen
the moans gave themselves over
to gritty rhythms that jigged and jived
around my tongue
keeping time
with the click click click of keyboard

Mountain streams once threatened
by drought flowed onto pages where
lilt and intonation scattered
where internal rhyme
was damned or blessed,
and now my friend
you know the rest.

Wound To Wing

I have come to believe
that these poems
all along

Have been tucked
delicately, deeply
within my
breastbone

And you, dear reader
let shine
unencumbered
a holy witness

Let us bless
this darkness spell
when soul was dimmed
where love felt sting

And so, pierced thus
with invited gaze
relinquish I
this wound,
to wing.

A special thank you to *Kathy Hellum* who
graciously shares in this book
her photography from her travels
as well as the beauty
of everyday life.
She lives with her husband in Seattle Washington

Kathy can be reached at kathyhellum@gmail.com

The

TRue

GIET

Love   is

hope

within

You

AllWa3

FORRest

I encourage all acts of poetic mischief and welcome your thoughts and making lifetime connections through poetry. To inquire about my poetry, sound and movement playshops, please find me online or email me at kristy. hellum@gmail.com

Printed in the United States
By Bookmasters